A SHARING BY
Father Bill Stelling

Eagle Wing Books, Inc.
Box 9972
Memphis, TN 38109

Published in the United States by Eagle Wing Books, Inc.

All inquiries should be addressed to:
Eagle Wing Books, Inc.
Box 9972
Memphis, TN 38109

ISBN: 0-940829-07-X

Retail Price: $9.95

First U.S.A. Printing: September 1992

ACKNOWLEDGMENTS

I am convinced that original thinkers are few and far between. Therefore, I am happy to acknowledge my debt to:

Anthony DeMello, S.J., who, with the wisdom and humor of his many stories (especially his *The Song of the Bird*, 1982) has helped me grow.

Justin J. Kelly, S.J., for his insightful article, FAITH: THE HUMAN DIMENSION, which appeared in *The Way*, July 1971.

Richard Rhor, ofm, through his many tapes, has long been a spiritual mentor for me. He has encouraged me to seek "truth speakers" in my life.

Austin Ripley, founder of Guest House, for his compelling description of gratitude which I have used with permission of Gust House.

Leonard Bernstein for *Singing God a Simple Song*.

The Saint Joseph Edition of *The New American Bible* as the source of the scriptural quotations I have used.

Archbishop Daniel M. Buechlein, O.S.B., D.D. whose intervention in my life wrought results I had never dared to dream of.

Dr. Greg Little, without whose help and support this

book would never have become a reality.

Bill W. and Dr. Bob who were not afraid to share with others what they had been given.

Family, Friends, and the People in the parishes in which I have served who, even now, are teaching me to be a pastor.

A special "Thank You," to Miss Brenda Adams, my secretary, for her hours of patient proof reading.

You have my thanks and my prayers.

Father Bill Stelling

TABLE OF CONTENTS

Fore Thoughts

B ecause I am a priest, many people have sought my advice on how to grow spiritually. Since my own spiritual life has so many ups and downs, I have been reluctant to give any advice. However, I have become convinced that it is important that we share our experiences, because I believe that spiritual growth is not something we do alone.

In this little volume, I have presented some of my thoughts on Spirituality. I call them my Spiritual Stumbling and Building Blocks. I have presented them simply because they are simple. They are also very common ingredients in my Spiritual Life.

Spirituality — Making it Simple

What is Spirituality, anyway? *Webster's Dictionary* tries to help us. I don't think he is a big help. He says it's 1) spiritual character, quality, or nature. 2) the jurisdiction, rights, tithes, etc. belonging to the church or an ecclesiastic. 3) the fact or state of being incorporeal (without a body).

He gives no better insight defining Spiritual: 1) of the spirit or soul. 2) concerned with the intellect. 3) consisting of spirit, not body. 4) showing much refinement of thought and feeling. 5) of the church or religion.

These complications remind me of the story, "The Little Fish," told by Anthony deMello in *The Song of the Bird*. I have rephrased it for my purposes.

A little fish in a large aquarium was observed by an older and wiser fish swimming rapidly back and forth across the tank. He swam up next to the little fish and asked, "What are you doing?"

"I was told that a fish needs water to live so I'm looking for the water."

The older fish was not surprised, he'd been through this before. "We're in the water, the water's all around us. That's what we're swimming in."

"You're kidding," said the little fish, with astonishment. "It can't be that simple." With that, he swam off to continue his search for the water.

Spirituality: An Awareness of God

Dictionaries and theologians may put it differently, but for me, Spirituality is simply becoming aware that God is all around me. The quality of my Spirituality goes up and down depending on how I let people, places, things, and events interfere with, or add to, my awareness of God.

Spiritual Basics

Keeping to basics, another question comes to mind. What or Who is God? Now there's a question a lot of ink and blood have been spilt over. I'm certain that there is a God and I'm just as certain that each of us understands God in a unique way. Let me share with you some of the things I understand about God.

I'm convinced that I'm not God. And I'm convinced that everything that exists, somehow, has its origin *in* God. I also believe that God actually loves me and invites me to share His life. From time to time, when my faith weakens, I wonder, "why?" Then, I realize that, although love does mean that I must say, "I'm sorry," now and then, love does not answer the question — "Why?" I believe the scripture that tells me that God is not *only* Love, but *also* Truth.

For me, the question, "How do I grow Spiritually?" is the same as asking, "How do I respond to God's invitation to share His life?" In the following pages I will share with you some stumbling blocks in my spiritual journey and some building blocks in my spiritual growth. I share these because I believe that we do not travel this journey alone. My spiritual life and yours are interrelated.

In the ancient world, and even in the Old Testament, numbers were often used as symbols. The number 6 was used as a symbol of imperfection, and 7 as a symbol of perfection. So I'll share with you six stumbling blocks and seven building blocks in my spiritual life. Rest assured that I encounter more than six stumbling blocks and I am aided by more than seven building blocks in my spiritual journey.

PART I

SIX STUMBLING BLOCKS
IN THE SPIRITUAL JOURNEY

1. Fear

2. Discouragement

3. Anger

4. Impatience

5. Complicating
   the Simple

6. Ego

Fear

The 1st Stumbling Block

Fear, now there's a trip. Fear comes in many guises. There is fear of the known and the unknown, fear of what others may think of me, and of what I will think of me, specific fear and non-specific fear.

Whatever guise fear appears under, it is Fool's Gold, it's a phony, it's a liar. It always seeks the easy way out. I'm not talking about prudence, nor caution, these are healthy. I'm talking about the kind of fear that endlessly questions every risk.

Playing Fear's Game

When I fall victim to fear, I'm unable to risk anything. Once I begin to play fear's game, I discover what addicts already know. One question, one doubt, one drink, one bite, one look is too much and a thousand are not enough.

Fear insists that I review a million options and will not permit me to select one. It brings darkness to light and confusion to order. It blocks any real spiritual growth and is a demon.

The stumbling block of fear pretends to be a child of reason, but is truly a bastard. It can have a physical effect on me. It settles like ice water in my bowels and leaves my mind in a fog. It can paralyze me with worry and deny value to any decision making process of mine.

Dealing With Fear

How to deal with this demon?

First, I believe that fear, especially unreasonable fear, is a tool of the devil and will always be at hand. However, this does not excuse me from taking steps to deal with it. **So I try to keep in mind that while fear is always waiting to emerge — I can cope with it.**

Second, when fear convinces me that my decisions will be imperfect, I try to remember that perfection is not a requirement for happy living. Very often making a mistake is a better option than doing nothing. **This is when it is especially helpful for me to talk things over with a friend.**

Third, I recall what Jesus told that despairing crowd before he restored the daughter of Jairus: **"Fear is useless, what is needed is trust."** Trust, or faith is what I need to deal with fear. As I strengthen my faith, I am better able to deal with it. I have found that the two best ways for me to strengthen my faith are: **Prayer to God and an honest sharing of my problem with other human beings.**

When I am in the grip of fear, I try to keep my prayer simple, direct and brief, but persistent. Fear makes it so easy for me to believe the negative and almost impossible to believe the positive. So when fear attacks, my prayer will often be, *"God, help me to know you love me, so we can get through this together."*

In recent years I have come to know the benefit of an honest sharing of my problems with people I respect and trust. I have come to accept, as primary truths, that there are few problems that cannot be helped by talking about them, and that most of the things I fear never come to pass. Whether or not these are primary truths is not half as important as the help they have given me in dealing with fear and in enhancing my spiritual growth.

Discouragement

Discouragement has been a major stumbling block on my spiritual journey and it is almost always an active partner of fear. To discourage means to take away a person's courage. The Latin word *cor*, from which our word courage springs, actually means heart. So, Discouragement is a Stumbling Block to Spiritual Growth because it robs a person of the heart to grow.

I fall victim to this demon in several ways. Sometimes I find it difficult to accept myself as a person who is permitted to make mistakes. Theoretically, I know that all people make mistakes. It's not that I think I'm too good to make mistakes.

It's just that from time to time I get down on myself for being so stupid. I get discouraged because of what I think of myself.

At other times the real or supposed criticism by others puts my weaknesses in a glaring light. Society scorns weakness and failure, so, fearing society's scorn or my own, I want to quit. Every slip, every weakness, every failure is seen as a reason to quit.

In Paul's writings I find a new way to live. "The Lord said to me, 'My grace is sufficient for you, for power is made perfect in weakness.' I will gladly boast of my weaknesses, in order that the power of Christ may dwell with me. Therefore, I am content with weaknesses, for when I am weak, then I am strong." *(2Cor. 12:9ff)*

Surrender and Become Strong

To see my weaknesses as a source of strength, rather than discouragement, is like stepping off into the darkness. It's a scary adventure. It seems like giving up, but it is a *surrender*.

To give up means to stop trying to grow. To surrender means to stop trying to grow alone. To surrender means to accept Spiritual Growth as a gift from the hands of God — not as a wage earned by the work of my hands.

How do I surrender? I have found three ways that work for me. **1) I talk to God, 2) I listen to God, 3) I talk and listen to God.**

When I talk to God, I pray. My prayer changes often according to my needs and moods. Sometimes it's Liturgical or memorized prayer. At times it is a song, then rambling personal conversations. It may be simply one or two words that mean more than I can say, and then it may be just quiet thoughts. Whatever it is, it is always a prayer for the gift of Hope — the flip side of discouragement.

When I listen to God I may read Scripture, or appreciate the beauty of nature. There are times when my dog, Jock, and I go for a walk.

When I talk and listen to God I am sharing joys, sorrows, thoughts and whatever with other people.

The common threads I see in dealing with this demon of discouragement are **my relationship with God through personal prayer and my relationship with God through other people**.

Anger

There is a difference between being angry and being mad. Here, when I say "mad," I also mean "angry."

I know that anger has some good and useful purposes. One of them is to prompt me to get off my apathy and do something about the injustices around me. But, here, let's look at anger only as a Stumbling Block to Spiritual Growth.

Anyone who fights fires knows that visible flames are not the only sign of fire or danger. I've learned that just because I'm not yelling or screaming doesn't mean I have no anger to deal with. I know that I can just as easily be angry at myself for making a mistake as I can be at others for a supposed hurt.

Have you ever tried to give a cat a bath? Picture in your mind that screaming, squalling, scratching cat. That's anger. When I'm angry, it makes no difference whether it's anger from resentments I hold on to for months, spur of the moment anger, or just mad at myself, it's like trying to give a cat a bath. It serves no good purpose, and I'm going to get hurt. I know that, but I forget it when somebody rattles my cage. When I calm down I ask myself, *"Why do I let anger claim such a big place in my life?"*

Here is an answer I've discovered. I hate to admit there's nothing I can do about a situation. The situation over which I have no control may be a person, place or thing. The cause of my lack of control may be inside or outside of me. **The point is, that I have no power — and I don't like it.**

Coping With Anger and Control Issues

What can I do? Two courses are open to me. I can seek help, or I can deny I have no control.

I've discovered that I can back up and increase this denial by getting angry. Getting angry gives me the *illusion* that I'm doing something, and therefore, still in control. It surprises me how often I fall for that lie. Anger clouds my judgement and blocks my Spiritual growth.

What can I do about the lie that anger tells me, and for which I so often fall? Well, I got several things going for me. *1) At least now, I'm aware of anger's deceitful little game. 2) I really want to grow beyond anger's lie. 3) I talk about it with a friend who is willing to listen, but not judge or indulge me. 4) I'm willing to be satisfied with growth, no matter how slow it is. 5) I'm convinced that my God loves me and has not given me a date on which I have to be done with anger.*

There's another kind of anger that's a real roadblock to my spiritual growth. This I call non-specific anger. Sometimes I just get up on the wrong side of the bed. At times some little thing sets me off and I'm not even aware of it til anger is in charge. To deal with non-specific anger I find the five actions I mentioned before to be helpful, but doing something — something physical, is better. Something like a walk in the woods, work in the garden — and even sitting down at my computer and writing about it.

Time is a teammate too, if I let it be. Used to be when I looked back on being angry, I'd get mad at myself for getting mad. Now, with time and friends I can talk to, I'm able to be happy with myself as a person who gets mad, or angry now and then.

In the next section I'll share with you some of the problems I have with patience. On my Spiritual Journey, anger and impatience are closely related.

Impatience

Impatience is a word that means to refuse to endure, or to suffer. Patience is not one of my outstanding virtues. At times I think that if I'd been working with God in the beginning, creation would have taken only one, not six, days.

For a long while, I thought of patience as a minor virtue and impatience as a minor vice. But I've come to realize that my impatience usually involves a dissatisfaction with, or rejection of, reality in ways great or small. Reality, whether I like it or not, is important because that's where God is.

According to me, I have two faults of impatience: Being stalled in traffic; and moving in traffic. According to many others, there is no way to keep track of the faults

I have of impatience. For me, where impatience is, anger is seldom far behind.

Stalling on the Spiritual Journey

Sometime ago I found myself stalled in a traffic jam. I'm not one of those people who lays on the horn. I just sit and fume. Quite by chance the voice on the radio announced the time and I glanced at the clock on my dashboard to see if it was right. It was that glance that led me to a startling discovery. I noted, when traffic began moving freely again, that less than three minutes had elapsed.

Most of my time in the car is spent alone, so there is no one to pass the time with. Perhaps that is fortunate. Since I made the discovery about the three minutes, I try to remember to have the *Reader's Digest* or a book of jokes or puzzles in the car with me. I find this helpful whenever I am waiting in line at the checkout counter, at the bank, and other places, too. I get some strange looks, but I just smile patiently.

When I'm impatient, it most often has to do with the passage of time. Time passes so slowly when all I have to do is wait. There's the saying, *"This too shall pass,"* of which I've never been too fond. Psalm 90 has some words of wisdom, "For a thousand years in Your sight are as yesterday, now that it is past, or as a watch of the night." If you've ever worked the night shift, you know how long it can seem, and how short it actually was, "Now that it is past."

There are many other things that I get impatient about. People who say, "You know," every other sentence. People who never come to the point. People who tell a joke and forget how it ends. But the worst offenders are time and traffic. I thought that was a short list, until a friend said, "Let's see now, you are impatient with people, time, and traffic, what are you patient *with*?"

Enduring Impatience and its Anger

In my Spiritual Journey I find that impatience often leads to anger, and neither impatience nor anger are good for my Spiritual Growth. **When I get impatient, it means that I am refusing to endure, to accept reality.** As the saying goes, I'm refusing to accept life on life's terms.

So what can I do? As soon as I become aware of the problem, I ask myself, "Who do you think you are, that you expect traffic, time, and people to respect your desires?" The answer I give myself is, "Well, I'm not God." This serves to break the tension and often brings a chuckle. **I find it more and more helpful in my spiritual growth to be able to laugh at myself.** Then, I try to turn to something to occupy my time, like the digest I mentioned.

Complicating the Simple

I'm like the Little Fish in the story I related in the Fore Thoughts. I have a real penchant for complicating simple things. I, and others, have asked, "Why?"

I guess there are as many answers to that question as there are occasions to ask it. It's a simple question and I'll try to honor it with simple answers. I'll answer it for myself. It would be wrong to try to answer for anyone else. If you find my insights help-ful, go for it.

Being a CAD

When I complicate the simple it's almost always because I'm being a CAD. That is, I'm Controlling,

*A*voiding, and *D*enying. CAD is an old word used to describe a man whose behavior is less than gentlemanly.

If I want to control a situation, all I have to do is complicate it. Then it becomes clear to me, and everyone else, that the situation needs controlling and no one is better suited than I to do it.

Simple things don't need controlling, they should be enjoyed. Sometimes I enjoy things so much I try to prolong them. That's control and it complicates things. Control complicates most things, especially love and friendship.

Even when I'm in charge, there's the urge to micromanage. I find this a quick and easy way to make a complicated mess of things. The lure that sucks me in is ego, and it usually backfires.

Another way I have of complicating simple things is avoiding them. I know there's a problem, but I avoid it. Maybe I don't like the pain, the embarrassment, the money, or the time it will cost me. Maybe, I hope, if I ignore it, it'll go away. That doesn't really work. It doesn't with a sore tooth, and it won't work if I'm overdrawn at the bank, either.

Denial is another of my ways of complicating the simple. The problem is, denial always makes my life so simple — for a while — and then there's hell to pay. A good thing that can be said for Denial is that it works, if even for a little while. But I know this: *denial complicates my life*. And the warranty on it always runs out. There comes a time I must admit that I'm playing games. At that point, my life has already become quite complicated.

Keeping the Simple – Simple

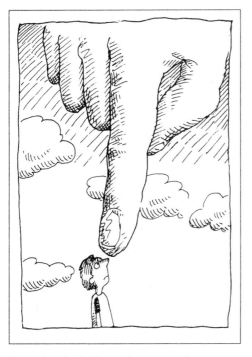

How can I keep from being a CAD, from Controlling, Avoiding, and Denying? How can I outsmart the devil and stop complicating the simple?

The first thing that works for me in simplifying matters is to recall what one of the Sisters told me in grade school. *"You can't outsmart the devil. So hide in God."* Today I know that means surrender to my God.

The devil's tool is complication, while God's is simplicity. In Leonard Bernstein's *"Mass,"* I hear words of both the poet and the theologian, *"Sing God a simple song. Make it up as you go along. God loves all simple things, for God is the simplest of all."*

In seeking to avoid complications, I search for little ways, for simple ways. I often fail, but when my mind is calm again, I try to hide in God. I hum a bit, and then I sing. I sing God a Simple Song.

Ego

Ego, like a temperature and an attitude, is common to us all. Yet when we're told, "You have a temperature, or an attitude, or an ego," it doesn't sound good. That's too bad, because without a temperature, we'd be dead. Without an attitude, we'd be unreal. Without an Ego, we'd be inhuman. None of those three conditions are good for living human beings.

When I Have PSI

When I say that Ego is a stumbling block in my spiritual growth, I'm referring to the times when I have *PSI*. PSI is Phony Self Image and it can be either too big or too little. Size is not the issue, phoniness is.

I resort to a PSI that's too little for me when I try to escape responsibility for something I've done by expressing an attitude typically stated, "Well, I'm only human." This is humility with a hook. And it sets aside the

Scripture I hold dear, that says God created us, male and female, in His own image.

I have it on good authority that human nature reflects the image of God. **So when I excuse my faults with, "I'm only human," I am not growing spiritually at all.** I've got an Ego problem.

I resort to a PSI that's too big for me when I try to escape responsibility for something I've done by adopting an attitude expressed in these or similar words, "Look, I've told you the best way to do it. If you can't accept that, that's your problem." That's pride, born of arrogance — not truth. And it limits the wisdom of God to me.

God has made each of us to reflect His image. So when I shut off the views of others because of my superior knowledge, I do not grow spiritually at all. I've got an Ego problem.

I am persuaded that God is Truth, and, for reasons of His own love, He has chosen to give Himself to me. So, no matter how hard I study or work, in the end, truth is a gift.

It is important for me to constantly remind myself of this, lest prompted by pride issuing from arrogance or false humility, I seek security in a PSI.

Ego abused, from left or right, is a PSI and it allows no spiritual growth. My inclination is to hide my weaknesses and flaunt my strengths, but this, too, is PSI.

Coping With Ego

What puts PSI to flight?

When I'm all wrapped up in a PSI it is helpful for me to ask myself some questions. **Is the truth less true when told by a fool? Is the truth less enlightening when told by an enemy? Is a lie less a lie because it flatters my ego? Is a lie less a lie because it's told by a scholar?**

It is also good for me to remember that bit of wisdom, old, yet ever fresh: **"To thine own self be true."** Simple to say, but oh, so very tough to do. For me it takes a daily

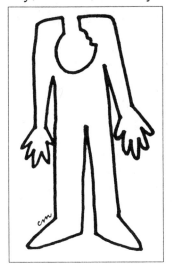

renewal of purpose. A continuous personal inventory or examination of conscious. Of particular importance to my Spiritual Growth is a willingness to forgive and to seek forgiveness. This is important, because when I strive to forgive and seek forgiveness, PSI ceases to have power over me. **Above all, overcoming PSI takes the help of God and neighbor.**

PART II

SEVEN BUILDING BLOCKS

1. Honesty

2. Prayer

3. Faith

4. Discipline

5. Coping — Acceptance & Letting Go

6. A Companion

7. Gratitude

Honesty

The Scripture tells me that God is Truth. When I write of Truth, I am writing of Honesty.

I believe that God has invited me to share His life. If I'm going to accept the invitation I have to begin by getting Honest. I'm not talking about "cash register" honesty, but I'm not excluding it, either.

I'm talking about that honesty that forces me to accept myself as I really am, warts and all. Honesty that forces me to face my relationship with God as it is, not as I or others think it should be. Honesty that requires me to look clearly at how I relate to others. It challenges me to confront my preconceived and com-

fortable notions. It calls me to face harsh truths rather than give into a lie for the sake of comfort or to avoid embarrassment.

It is so easy to manipulate truth, especially when I want to do something I know I shouldn't. A good example of the manipulation of truth to preserve the appearance of honesty can be seen in the account of David's affair with Bathsheba. But be sure to see how he got honest when confronted with his dishonesty. *(2 Sam. chapter 11 through chapter 12:15)*

Honesty is Light

Honesty gives light to the very essence of my soul. But if I close the eyes of my soul, then my soul becomes a dark and shallow place. Honesty, if it is to be meaningful, must be a way of life, and not something I do now and then.

In my experience I must acknowledge that fear is a powerful enemy of honesty. Reason and experience tell me that I will survive if I "suck it up," and face an issue honestly. Fear does strange things to honesty. With great ease fear can turn reason into rationalizing, and experience into memories of failures.

Getting Honest

How do I get honest and strive to be honest in all areas of my life? Honesty was neither conceived nor born in a vacuum. God is its progenitor and fellowship is its midwife. God and fellowship are distinct, but as the old song goes, *"You can't have one without the other."* For me this means **if I am going for total honesty, I must talk about this in prayer with God, and share the problem with at least one other human being who will be a "truth speaker" in my life.**

Being honest in all the areas of my life can be tough now and then. Sometimes the things that give me the most trouble are the little things. I keep trying to tell myself, "This is not important, it won't make any difference."

Then, I ask myself, "Are you going to make yourself a liar for something that's not important?" Being honest doesn't get easier, but if I work at it, I'll get stronger.

Prayer

It seems to me that if I am going to have a relationship with another person, then I'm going to have to get to know that person. Even, in fact, especially, if that person is God.

This brings up a question. What is the purpose of

prayer? Well, there are prayers of Praise, Thanksgiving, Petition, Contrition, etc. Beyond all of that I think that prayer is a means of communication — rooted in faith. Without faith, prayer is just hypocrisy. No matter what else prayer is, it is a means of communication.

An Invitation for Communication

Lovers and other people communicate. They talk for hours on the phone, they write letters, they communicate with a glance, an embrace, or simply holding hands. Why? There are many reasons, but when you get to the bottom line, the purpose is to get to know each other. I think that getting to know God is, or should be, the primary purpose of prayer. I believe that God loves me, and invites me to share His life. My prayer is an important response to that invitation.

There are different types of prayer, ranging from memorized to contemplative. I used to advise people to study the different types and choose one they felt comfortable with. I don't do that anymore. I don't think the way I pray should be simply a matter of picking and choosing. I believe the type of prayer I use is a gift, and it changes from time to time. I don't think that one type of prayer is better than another. It's not a matter of rank, it is a matter of gift.

I know some people, myself included, whose morning prayer is, from time to time, simply, *"Please,"* and whose night prayer is, *"Thank You."* **For the most part, I try to**

keep my prayer simple, brief, and persistent. I try to get to know God, who loves me. I take an example from human life. The conversation between human lovers may, at first, be stilted and even embarrassing, but if it's true love, it becomes natural and easy.

Getting to Know God

Prayer is a powerful and necessary building block in the Spiritual Life. I have learned that, if I predetermine what the answer to prayer must be, then I might just miss the answer I get. I might even decide that God has not answered my prayer, because He did not answer it in the way I told Him to.

With all the different types of prayer, and the many different ways of praying, prayer can be confusing. A bit of advice someone gave me applies here: When things are confused, reduce them to their simplest terms. What scripture says about prayer is very simple. Daniel 3:39 says, "A heart contrite and humbled, O, God, you will not spurn." In Romans 8:26 I find, "The Spirit too helps us in our weakness, for we do not know how to pray as we ought."

Praying Teaches Us How to Pray

I learn to pray by praying. The more I pray, the better I know how to pray and the better I know this God who loves me. The better I know this God who loves me, the more I want to pray and to share the life He offers me. It works for me. Try it, it might work for you.

Faith

Someone once told me that an act of faith is "the assent of the intellect to truths revealed by God because it is God who has revealed them." I'm not sure who told me that, but it had to be a theologian. Nobody else talks like that. I'm not going to argue with it. It's too abstract for me.

It seems to me that if I'm going to talk about the faith of everyday people it can't be limited to the intellect assenting to anything, firmly or otherwise. Faith, as a building block in my Spiritual Life, must relate to the whole person, not just the mind, but to the heart, not just the intellect, but to feelings as well. My mind can give assent to the fact that God is transcendent, which means totally other, but that doesn't impress me. What impresses me, what excites me, is that **this Transcendent God loves me**.

Belief in God

If I'm going to believe in God, and I do, then it has to be more than abstract theological faith. If I'm going to believe in God, and I do, that faith is going to have to give real meaning to my life. Let me share with you what it means to me to believe in God, to believe that God actually loves me.

First, I'm convinced that, in ordinary circumstances, faith in God is rarely simply a matter between me and God. I think that faith is a gift, but it is born in a family, and is nourished in fellowship, and community.

What has family, fellowship, and community got to do with my faith in God?

Some twenty years ago I read an article, FAITH: THE HUMAN DIMENSION, by Justin J. Kelly, in THE WAY, a Jesuit publication. He says: *"to believe in God as the fulfillment of one's life, without some experience of human and earthly fulfillment, would seem to be a psychological impossibility."* He also points out that this experience of human fulfillment starts with parents. They share with their children security, love, and the reality of their faith.

There are parents who offer their children no security, no love, and no faith. There are people who live their whole lives lacking even the most meager necessities for a good life. There are people who have never known and will never know the basic human rights of life, liberty, and the pursuit of happiness. Faith is a Di-vine gift practiced by human beings. Kelly says, *"Faith originates in an awareness that life is good."* Then he asks, *"What happens when life is not perceived as good?"*

Therein lies the role of family, fellowship, and community and my role as part of it. I have faith, but without works, faith is dead. For me this means that I have a responsibility to say and do the things that proclaim that life not only can be, but should be, good. I must make it known that the dignity of the human person should be more compelling than the profit motive. I, and perhaps you too, have heard people say in the midst of the radiance of nature, a sunset, the beauty of spring or fall, the power of the seas, the majesty of the mountains, **"How can anyone on seeing this not believe in God?"**

Is Life Burdensome?

For those who find life burdensome, I believe that any deliberate deed of living faith is more convincing than all the flowers and all the trees, than all the suns that rise and set, than all the mountains and all the seas that awe the human mind, for nature acts without a mind or will or heart. **But humankind with mind and will and heart join with God and announce that God, indeed, does love us, and that life can and should be good.** And our acts — our deliberate deeds — showing faith, announces God's love and the underlying goodness of life.

Discipline

For me, one of the most surprising Building Blocks of Spiritual Growth is discipline. It just never occurred to me that discipline had anything to do with Spirituality. I used to feel that if there was one place that a person should be free of all the restraints of discipline, it was in the Spiritual life.

I don't remember who got my attention or how, but today I think more realistically about the subject. I'm convinced, now, that without discipline there's likely to be little or no growth in the Spiritual Life. After all, if I'm seeking a relationship with God, I'm destined to become a disciple of God. The very word, "disciple," is essentially related to the word discipline.

Webster's Dictionary says that discipline is: 1) a branch of knowledge or learning; 2) training that develops self-control, character, orderliness and efficiency. Many people identify discipline only with military life. But there is discipline in the Spiritual Life. It is not the discipline that molds a person into a machine blindly following orders. It's the discipline that is the foe of self-centeredness. It is the discipline that enables a person to be truly free.

Discipline — A Means to an End

Discipline is a means to an end, not an end in itself. Self-control, or controlling others, is not the true end of discipline. I think the purpose of discipline is captured best by Francis Thompson in his *Ode to the English Martyrs*: **"Hardest servitude has he that's jailed in arrogant liberty; but freedom, spacious and unflawed, who is walled about with God."**

Discipline Fosters Freedom

Discipline is necessary for me in my Spiritual Growth. It is required by me to curb my appetite for the soft and easy way of life that Thompson refers to as "arrogant liberty." It is that practice which enables me to read and study, lest I be shackled by errors of the past. It frees me from the bondage of resentments and grudges by empowering me to forgive and eventually let go of personal hurts. It enables me to return to my prayer, even after the umpteenth distraction. I find it absolutely necessary to discipline myself to set aside a regular time for personal prayer. If I did not have this discipline, I would not have the freedom for personal prayer.

It is not difficult to keep a regular time for my public prayer life since it is regulated by a posted schedule. Discipline is necessary, however, to keep it from becoming routine. Discipline is necessary to keep my ego intact, when I hear comments from people either praising or condemning the way I pray publicly. Discipline is necessary for me to turn away temptations of letting my public prayer become a public display.

Getting Discipline:
A Decision, a Willingness, a Schedule

Discipline is an absolute requirement if I am going to maintain a private, or personal prayer life. I have found that there are three things I must do to get discipline in my life: **1) I must decide what is important for my spiritual** growth; 2) I must be willing to sacrifice to maintain priorities; 3) I must keep to the schedule.

I am persuaded that discipline is the chaperon of all the other Building Blocks of the Spiritual Life. It is also the bastion of the defense against Stumbling Blocks in Spiritual Growth. I must constantly be reminded that, although I strive for union with my Spiritual God, I am a creature of both spirit and flesh and while the spirit is willing, the flesh is weak.

Coping:
Acceptance & Letting Go

When I was a child my playmates and I played a game we called, "Tin Like." Most every child has played it. The game would usually begin when someone would say, "You tin like you're the sheriff and I'll tin like I'm the bank robber." Or, "I'll tin like I'm the Lone Ranger, and you tin like you're the bad guy."

Though the names and titles have changed, I like to think that children still play that game. Imagination can be fun and healthy and should be encouraged in both children and adults. There is a danger, however, that

children and adults may seek to exchange reality for "tin like," since "pretending like" often seems more comfortable. When this happens, I think the danger is more serious for adults than for children, since children usually grow out of it, while adults grow into it.

Coping With Real Life

Acceptance of Reality and Letting Go of "Tin Like," are building blocks in my Spiritual Life. Together they form one building block called *coping*. At times it's pleasant, at other times, it's harsh. The more I learn to Accept and Let Go, the more I grow. The more I avoid accepting reality or letting go of "tin like," the less I grow. **Coping is what I need to learn.** I already know enough about avoiding.

The concept of "Letting Go" is simple, but at times Letting Go is like a bug trying to let go of the spider's web. **My problems with Letting Go often deal with resentments and obsessions.** These are built up one day at a time, so when I Let Go, I most often have to **do it one day at a time.** If I try to grow spiritually while holding on to obsessions and resentments, it's like trying to light a match in a windstorm.

Letting Go

How does one, "Let Go?" This is different for each person. For me, there are some basics. *1) I have to really want to let go (desire). 2) I have to be willing to let go (readiness). 3) When I become aware that I'm dwelling on what I want*

to let go of, I try to do three things: pray; relax; pay more attention to what I should be doing (action). So, for me, **Letting Go requires desire, readiness, and action.**

Acceptance

Acceptance — the other biggie. How difficult it is to accept the unfairness, the wrongness, the injustice of life, especially when I know my way is fair, right, and just. That's the heart of the Serenity Prayer that I, and many others, have found useful in working on acceptance.

Does acceptance mean that I have to accept unfairness, injustice, and wrongness in this world? **Of course it does. God does! Do I have to be happy with it? No, but I can be serene with it. Serenity doesn't come from happiness, happiness comes from serenity. Spiritual Growth doesn't come from happiness. Happiness comes from Spiritual Growth.**

How do I grow in acceptance? First, by focusing on the fact that acceptance does not mean approval. Next, by remembering what a friend, Sean, told me, "Whatever you deal with can never get any better until it's okay just as it is." This is living the Serenity Prayer:

> *"God grant me serenity to accept what I can not change, courage to change what I can, and wisdom to know the difference."*

Finally, I must realize that the solution to most difficulties comes one day at a time, with the help of God, by sharing with others, and using my many failures as opportunities rather than obstacles.

A Companion

Among the blessings I find in my Church are the sponsors at Baptism and Confirmation. Unfortunately, sponsors are not always all they could and should be. For example, I don't recall ever getting to know my sponsors. This is unfortunate, but not uncommon. Of late, sponsorship is being seen not simply as an honor given, but as a relationship to be established.

As an adult pilgrim on a Spiritual Journey, I have enjoyed much benefit from having Spiritual Directors and regular confessors. There was a time when I thought this practice should be reserved for priests, sisters, brothers, or religious fanatics. I no longer think this is true.

In the last few years of my Spiritual Journey I've become convinced that I want and need something more than what I've had. I need more than I got from Baptismal and Confirmational Sponsors. I want more than I've received from Spiritual Directors and regular Confessors.

Much of my thinking on this has been formed by what I've learned about Twelve Step Recovery Programs and the process through which adults enter the Catholic Church, known as RCIA *(Rite of Christian Initiation for Adults)*.

In RCIA each adult has a sponsor and I've seen beautiful and lasting Spiritual Companionships develop from this. I have also seen deep Spiritual Relationships blossom between a Sponsor and sponsoree in Twelve Step Recovery Programs.

My vision of a *companion* for my Spiritual Journey takes elements from the roles of Spiritual Director and the regular Confessor. It also borrows from the ideal Sponsors at Baptism, Confirmation, RCIA, and Recovery Programs.

A Companion — A Sharing Relationship

The word Companion actually means to share bread with another. Bread is, to much of the world, the Staff of Life. With a Spiritual Companion I share, not just life, but Life in Abundance.

For some, the essence of a Spiritual relationship is centered in shared prayer. This is well and good for some,

but not for me, at this time. *Spirituality is about life.* Prayer is but one part of life. Much of my prayer life involves public prayer, so I enjoy, and jealously guard, my personal prayer times.

I used to have just one Spiritual Companion, now I have several. They do not ask, "How are you doing?", as a social question, they really want to know.

Share the Important Things

I used to talk to friends at great length and with authority about important things, such as, the National Debt, What the Communists were up to, Politics, and on and on. Now I talk to friends, Spiritual Companions, about truly important things such as, What I'm afraid of, What I'm happy about, What's upsetting my serenity, How my day has been. And I'm learning to listen to my friends for these important things. These are the really important things. I've discovered that the National Debt or What the Communists are up to don't help my Spiritual

Growth at all. **But by paying attention to my serenity and the serenity of others, I can begin to grow.**

Spiritual Companions are building blocks in my Spiritual Life because they speak the truth to me and listen for it from me. I once was told that people are only as sick as their secrets. Spiritual Companions keep me well. When I share my secrets, or whatever is worrying me, they lose power over me. A Spiritual Companion is truly a blessing from God.

Gratitude

Gratitude is the Crown Jewel of all the Building Blocks in the Spiritual Life. There are many definitions of Gratitude. One that has great meaning for me was written by Austin Ripley for recovering Alcoholics. I believe that it can apply to each person, since we are all recovering from something, even if just from the effects of sin.

"Gratitude is the memory of the heart. That quality which enables a man to double his fortune by sharing it. It is the Golden Tray on which we give to another the things we have received from God. The measure of a good A.A., lies not in what he knows, but in what he does. Not in how he thinks, but in what he feels. The assessment of a good A.A. is made, not in the brilliance of his mind, but in the charity of his heart. His stature is not gauged by how high he will reach to receive, but how low he will stoop to serve. A good A.A. is thankful, not only for what he has got, but he is grateful for what he can give. He strives not for cleverness, but for wisdom. He would rather be right, than popular. A good A.A. uses not the toughness of his mind, but the gentleness of his touch in bringing hope to the sick alcoholic. For he knows that if ever the lamp of his charity burns dim, the light of another alcoholic may go out forever.

We, who when we came into A.A. were not trusted by man in
the most trivial affairs of life, now are trusted by God in one of
the most important missions on earth — trusted by Him to
preserve and pass on this mighty miracle of sobriety to the
alcoholic who still suffers."

The Gospel of Luke (17:11-19) reports that Jesus cured
ten lepers but that only one returned to give thanks. Jesus
asked, "Were not all ten made whole? Where are the other
nine?" Verse 15 gives me an important insight. "One of
them, *realizing that he had been cured* came back ..."

The one discovered that he had been cured. He real-
ized that God had been at work in his life. The other nine
did not. Why? What blocked their attention to the simple
fact that God was at work in their lives? **The mind is
shocked by the terrible reality that the Giver of the gift
is forsaken in favor of the gift.**

Keep an Attitude of Gratitude

Bob, a friend of mine, often gives me the reassuring
advice, "Everything's gonna be fine, long as you got an
attitude of gratitude." Many of us go through life not
realizing the miracles God works in our lives. The making
of a mental "Gratitude List" at least once a month and a
written one with each change of seasons, helps me maintain
an "Attitude of Gratitude." Using the alphabet, I go from
"A" to "Z" and list the things I have simply because God
is God. If I can't think of anything for "Z," I use zygote,
without which I wouldn't be here.

**Gratitude is that marvel that enables me to appreciate
the Giver of the gift as superior to the gift that is given.**
It is that virtue that attracts me to the Giver beyond the

gift. The gift is Life, the Giver is Life in Abundance. Humanity is Life, Spirituality is union with Life in Abundance.

The story of the ten lepers teaches me to seek union with Life in Abundance by being constantly aware of the gifts I have received, and by looking beyond them to the Giver of all gifts.

An Attitude of Gratitude, *"Don't leave home without it."*

After Thoughts

I n my Fore Thoughts I mentioned that the reason for using only six Stumbling Blocks and seven Building Blocks was the symbolism given those numbers in ancient numerology. With this scheme I end up with 6 + 7, which equals 13. That's not a good number to end on, so I add a few After Thoughts.

There are, of course, many other Stumbling and Building Blocks that I could have mentioned. My intention was not to make an end of it, but to make a beginning. There is no end to the list, but unless there is a beginning there will never be any growth. Feel free to come up with Stumbling and Building Blocks of your own. Not to make an end, but to make a continuation.

A friend, who reviewed my manuscript, said, in dismay, "You've left out Love, which is the greatest Building Block of all."

I did leave it out, but I did so with design. **Love is the greatest Building Block. It is also the most obvious and**

the most inclusive. I think that all of the Building Blocks I've mentioned could easily fit under the title of Love. My design was not that it be left out, but that it be discovered in all the others.

There is an act of love that I have found indispensable for my Spiritual Growth: *forgiveness.*

Forgiveness is one of the necessary actions in letting go of something. It means to give up a resentment, to stop being angry with, to pardon, to give up all claim to punish or exact a penalty. To forgive does not mean to relieve one of the personal responsibility for moral rectitude, this would be enabling. To forgive means not to hold a grudge. This is healing. There is a saying, *"To err is human, to forgive is Divine."* It is easy for me to see that Forgiveness is a Spiritual Building Block. **The struggle is to forgive, as God forgives me**.

In my Church we have a Sacrament, variously called, Confession, Penance, or Reconciliation. It is important to note the way the Sacrament is celebrated. First there is Confession. That is, a person acknowledges, with sorrow, personal sin. Then there is forgiveness. Then there is Penance. Look at the way Jesus forgives sin. I do not recall any time that Jesus ever said, "If you do penance, I'll forgive your sin." No, it was always the faith of the person, the forgiveness of Jesus, and His manifest love that enabled the person to do penance. That is the way the Church celebrates the Sacrament.

There are two mistakes I am subject to when I have trouble forgiving a person who injures me. At times I insist on some repayment, some sign of repentance before I forgive. At other times I forgive in an enabling way that robs a person of personal responsibility for growth. When I look at Jesus, I see that while He holds a person accountable to grow, it is His forgiveness and manifestation of love that enables that person to grow and make some repayment, some sign of repentance. When I strive to forgive as Jesus did, I find true Spiritual Growth.

At the beginning I said that my Spiritual Growth is not something I do alone. I find Spiritual Growth comes most naturally for me when I listen to and share with others. For me it is the only source of true and lasting happiness. Trying to use the Building Blocks, and to overcome the Stumbling Blocks, is a task to be accomplished for me, not a goal achieved. Sometimes nothing seems to go right and everything seems to go wrong. I just want to quit. It's then that I hear a voice within me, **"Power is made perfect in weakness. Don't quit. Just surrender one day at a time."**

NOTES

NOTES